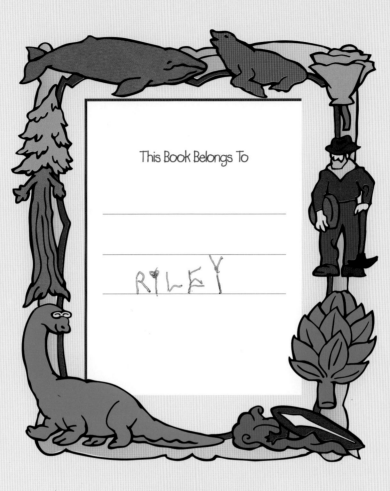

This Book Belongs To

RILEY

California

ABC

Copyright © 1997
Original Illustrations by Tim Mitoma
Concept and Text by Michelle McD-Furuichi
Type is Modern Twenty & Lemonade

Library of Congress Catalog Card Number: 97-91109

ISBN 0-9660593-1-X

Published by
kibō™

Printed in Korea

Distributed by Smith News Co. Inc.
460 Ninth Street
San Francisco, CA 94103
(415) 861-4900

BY **Michelle McD-Furuichi & Tim Mitoma**
ILLUSTRATED BY **Tim Mitoma**

an ANT bumps into a Redwood Tree

Bb

a BUMBLEBEE enjoys a picnic in Napa

Cc

a COW watches protons race at Stanford

Dd

a DINOSAUR swims in the La Brea Tar Pits

8

Ee

an ELEPHANT drives along the Pacific Highway

9

Ff

a FROG jumps at Angels Camp

Gg

a GORILLA climbs the Golden Gate Bridge

Hh

a HIPPO pumps iron at Venice Beach

Ii

an IGUANA tiptoes through Death Valley

13

Jj

Father JUNIPERO SERRA sells sandals at
Carmel Mission

Kk

a KITE flies over the red-tiled rooftops of Santa Barbara

a LLAMA carries a pack to the top of Mt. Shasta

Mm

a MONSTER compares chips in Silicon Valley

Nn

a NYMPH serves breakfast to a sleeping bear
at a B&B in Mendocino

an OCTOPUS shops in Beverly Hills

19

Pp

a POPPY leads the parade through California

a QUASAR dances for the telescope at
Griffith Observatory

a RACCOON scales the frontside of Half Dome in Yosemite National Park

a SEA OTTER swims in Monterey Bay

Tt

a **TUG BOAT** pulls a banana past the
Pigeon Point Lighthouse

Uu

an UNDERWATER SERPENT swims in Lake Tahoe

Vv

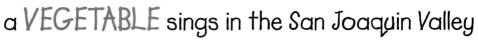

a *VEGETABLE* sings in the San Joaquin Valley

Ww

a WEASEL visits the Capitol in Sacramento

Xx

an X marks the spot at Sutters Mill

a YELLOW JACKET plays golf in Palm Springs

Zz

a ZOO full of animals in San Diego

ABCDEFGHIJKLM

NOPQRSTUVWXYZ

. . . but now, a Good Night and Sleep Tight.

"See Ya Later Pachyderm"

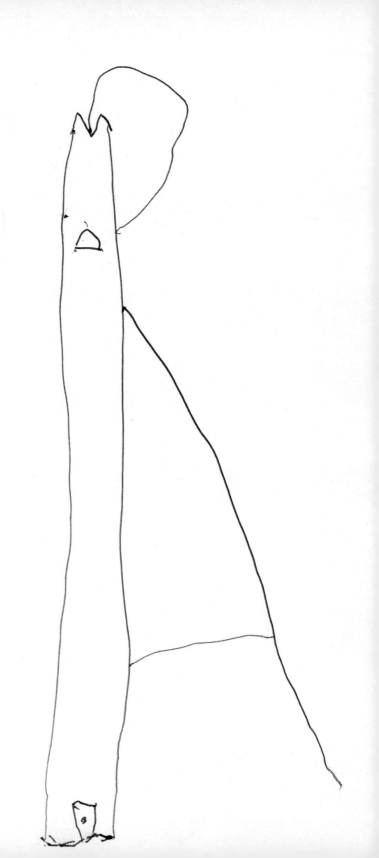

A   B   C

D   E   F

G   H   I   J

K   L   M